THE AUTOBIOGRAPHY OF
THOMAS LEONARD MITCHELL

THE AUTOBIOGRAPHY OF
THOMAS LEONARD MITCHELL

DO YOU KNOW WHO I AM?
"I AM THE GOAT"
The Roads I Traveled Led To The Steps I Took

THOMAS MITCHELL

Library of Congress Control Number:		2021915737
ISBN:	Hardcover	978-1-6641-8800-6
	Softcover	978-1-6641-8799-3
	eBook	978-1-6641-8798-6

Print information available on the last page.

Rev. date: 08/04/2021

To order additional copies of this book, contact:
Xlibris
844-714-8691
www.Xlibris.com
Orders@Xlibris.com
832804

First giving honor and thanks to my Lord, Savior and Redeemer. This book has two folds to why I wrote it. First a Purpose and second a Reason. I dedicate this book to my family, whose love and patience has made my life complete and gives me the inspiration to dig deep within myself to share my story with others so it might encourage and be the instrument they need to live their best Life.

To my Mother who carried me in her bosom for nine months, nurturing, caring for me and providing the necessary ingredients to be born healthy and well. To my Father, my father who is now deceased thanks for giving me Life to enter into this world and the guidance and instructions to the best you could give a son. To my siblings John my eldest brother who is now deceased, my eldest sister Mary, my sister Elaine, my brother Kelvin, my sister Doretha who is now deceased, my sister Carolyn, my youngest brother Henry O'Neal and my youngest sister Venita growing up with all of you definitely instilled in my life the importance of sharing, loving and life lessons that provided the foundation I needed to learn, live and to listen to myself while watching and learning from your (ours) lives growing up together. Thanks you all for all your Love, much love in return.

To my children eldest daughter Tanisha, my eldest son Thomas Jr, my son Tyren and my youngest daughter Karis. I could not have been blessed more with any better children than you all. Each of you are unique in your own way, I love and cherish each of you until my last breath and eternity. To my granddaughter Sophee who is my first grandchild who stole my heart and intentionally allowed me to spoil her rotten. You are so smart, witty and loving. I can see you being the first female president. To my grandson Leo Thomas who is my second grandchild, you have the heart of a lion and the most handsome look of a Prince, I am glad you are in my life I can see you doing and accomplishing great things. To my grandson Tacar I have not spent a lot of time with you but I have seen your growth from pictures and postings from your mom. I know you also will grow up to do great things.

Lastly, my dear Wife Karen, I saved you for last since you are the one whom I have known for 35 years and married to for 31 years at the time of me writing this book. Basically I have been with you all my whole adult life. You have been my rock; you give me breath and take my breath away all at the same time. 100% devoted and dedicated; No matter what I set my mind and heart to do you has always challenged me to do my very best, and always advise me to pray through problems. To my Readers, this is my belief and please don't think that in any way I am comparing my wife to God. However, I have been taught as a little boy and as I have grown up in church that God / Lord / Jesus is the one who gives LIFE. I have been taught that God / Lord / Jesus is love, peace, hope, God / Love / Jesus forgives, give second chances, God / Lord / Jesus will bless you. Well my wife Karen also gave life now listen; I know that to be true because I witnessed all the births of my children, also my wife have all the adjectives and attributes I just named. So I am not calling her God but a GODDESS.

Karen taught me that being a participant in a relationship/ partnership is not the same as being in a committed relationship. The breakup, separation and divorce rate is at an all time high, when you are committed the narrative change to OURS. For example our children, our problems, our solutions, our stress, our bills, our money, our success, our health, our failures, our business, our sickness, our wellness, our health, our Life. I am in no way shape or form trying to come across as the author of relationships but 31 years of marriage to the same person will teach you the principle of becoming as One. I am definitely blessed to have met, married and spent my whole life with her.

My Definition of Friendship:

My true circle is small. I have many acquaintences, people that I know and people that know me over the years. I had basically two child hood friends while living in Hartwell Georgia. James "Beanie Thornton (deceased--RIP), Randy "Hank" Rucker. We always ran together, hung out together chased young ladies together.

My military and current friends that I categorize as two types: Good Friend/Best Friend and Certified Friend.

AvanOwens- Good Friend / Best Friend – I met in the military at Fort Hood, Texas, we served in the same unit. Owens is my best friend for many reasons. He would give the shirt off his back if I needed it or asked for it. We also worked in the prison in Shelby County Tennessee and spent time with our families together. We keep in touch to this day.

Lambert Chatman-Certified Friend-I met Chatman while working at the Shelby County Prison, we served in the air force, police department and shared so many memories and experiences throughout our lives. Chatman is certified because he will always go that extra mile to make sure things are good. Chatman always keeping touch and shows genuine concern for me and my family, I can call upon him for anything and he would come through.

Your royal name, your bloodline, your position, your class, your title, your occupation, your degrees, your race/ ethnicity will never tell the true PERSON you really ARE.

Do you know who I Am?

What is Your Life's Blueprint?

I am a Student, College Graduate, Director, Manager, Military Soldier, Correctional Officer, Police Officer, Buffalo Soldier, Federal Agent, Business Owner, Inspiring Actor, Consultant, Public Speaker, Security Director, Bodyguard, Private Investigator, Detective, Security Consultant, White Collar Worker, Blue Collar Worker, Husband, Father Brother, Uncle, Son, Cousin, and a True Believer.

TABLE OF CONTENTS

INTRODUCTION

Is someone making your life miserable?

Do people want you to show recognition to them?

Do people because of their position try to make you feel powerless?

Let's just say it is a fine line between respect and disrespect.

This is a book that will show you the ways I used to take myself forward.

You must learn about yourself. 'who "YOU" are? How YOU can find courage to take charge of your life.

Do you know who I am? Is a question that people of status has used for centuries. In movies and real life, at times when well to be figure heads, movie stars, celebrities, well known politicians, professional athletes and famous people in general might get pulled over by a police officer and say Do You Know who I am? They pull their weight to get out of trouble, out of a speeding ticket or arrest and they threaten to make one phone call and get people fired, reassigned or promoted or demoted. People that are in leadership positions often flex their weight and say Do you know who I am to people or staff who doesn't recognize their position of authority or position of status AS THE CEO OF THE CORPORATION.

Staffers or employees that work for famous people has walked up to workers and staff members in hotels, churches, bars, concerts, airline/ airplanes and ask do you know who that is? And verbally tell them this is Mr. Blank, Miss Blank, Actor blank, Rapper blank Senator Blank you get the picture in order to get the desired outcome.

The PURPOSE for writing this book was because everyone I meet or have met that know my story and the places I have traveled, jobs I have worked said man you should write a book, because no one can tell your story to your kids and grand kids the way you would and if you died your story would be lost. The REASON for writing this book is because I never knew much about my parents or grandparents life during their young years as children, what jobs, hobbies, places they traveled, how they met, what jobs they had. So it was important for me to change the narrative and to leave my foot print for my family and beyond to know who their father, husband, grandfather, friend and co- worker is and were. The clique "Talk about getting information straight from the horses mouth" Well my advice to you my readers is do not pass up the opportunity to ask your father, mother, sister, brother, (grandfather) paw paw, (grandmother)maw maw, daughter, son, friend the questions while they are alive. As you know no one knows the time or day when life is over so don't take the chance on missing the chance to get the information because no one can tell their story better than the person themselves.

MY CHILDHOOD

My name is Thomas Leonard Mitchell; I was born the fourth child; three brothers and four sisters, my father John Thomas Mitchell and mother Sue Nell Mitchell. I was born in Chicago, Illinois at Cook County Hospital. We moved to the State of Georgia a small town called Hartwell, Georgia, Hart County when I was very young around 5 years old. Hartwell Georgia is a small tourist town who motto is "The Best Town By a Dam Site. Hartwell has a huge Dam and reservoir is surrounded by huge lake called Lake Hartwell that you can see on some outdoors television channels when they are showing professional fishing. Hartwell boast about its outdoor recreational picnic areas, camp grounds and cabins. These It is managed by the United States Corps of Engineers.

I attended Zion CME church, I had to walk about a mile every Sunday to attend bible study and church services, and

I mostly went without siblings and attended by myself. I remember my very first bible schools home work assignment. It was the letters on the cross and what they stood for INRT0 in latin it meant leves Nazarenvs Rex Ivdaeorvn. However in the english translation it meant Jesus of Nazareth, the King of the Jews. I attended Hartwell elementary, middle school and Hartwell Bulldogs High School. My hobbies are horseback riding, playing raquetball, hanging out and traveling with my family. I played basketball and football in high school. Our house was about about a 3rd of a mile for where we had to walk to catch the bus for school. Sometimes in the middle of the night our cows, calf or horses would get loose and I as a kid would be up on a late night looking for them and still had to get to bed and go to school the next morning. As a young boy we lived on several acres of land. The part of the town we lived in was called Color Zion consisted on pastures with red dirt and gravel roads. We had a large farm with horses, cows, calf's, chickens that laid eggs for our meals, rooster, hogs, pigs that we slaughtered for our meats, we had a mule that I plowed our gardens that produced vegetables such as squash, peas, tomatoes, corn, potatoes and several other vegetables. We had beagle dogs my father was an avid hunter. We had several houses on our land.

Our house I lived in, my grandparent's house and my Uncle David house was all within the same areas, we had a huge barn, we had two out houses as our restrooms due to no running water but later we did get running water inside all houses. We had wood burning stoves, so I had to learn how to chop wood, We had a well that I remember had stopped up and my father lowered me approximately 20 feet down into this well to scoop out the dirt and mud to get the water pump started again, this was one of the scariest times of my life as a10 year old. We owned a John Deere tractor and we had big gardens where we grew our own vegetables such as squash, peas, tomatoes, okra and many others.

My father also owned an adult male baseball team and a adult female softball team, we had a full size baseball field on our property, we played against other cities and counties, we had a concession stand that my mother and sisters worked in during games selling hot dogs, chips, beer and sodas. I and my brothers were ball boys which required us to go find baseballs when they were foul or home runs were hit out of the fence. We also were the cleanup crew after games. My parents always provided well for us, Christmas was always toys, bicycles etc etc.

As I became around 13 or 14 years of age I started cutting grass for the rich or should I say well off people up town, I worked in chicken houses, loading hay, I picked cotton for a old man name Mr. Will, my mother made me a bag out of a pillow case and tied it with a string, I got smart one day realizing that I would get paid more by the weight so I started putting rocks in the bottom but one day Mr. Will caught on and said that could catch the cotton gin on fire. So that was the last day I picked cotton. I got a summer job with the Corps of Engineers helping the crews spray the rocks around the dam with weed killer, help fix lantern poles, picnic grills etc etc. When I turned 16, I worked at the textile mill loading bundles and spools of cloth from machines. My grandparents were bootleggers our town at the time was what we called a dry county so no alcohol was sold at stores.

If you wanted to get any alcohol you were required to go across the river / bridge into South Carolina. My grandparents hid pints of liquor and beer in the woods in burlap bags. On the weekdays and mostly weekends especially after ballgames they would sell the alcohol, also there was a lot of gambling and disturbances and fights that I witnessed as a kid. There was a local general store not far from my house that gave my family The Mitchell's store credit I could go up to the store for my parents to get cigarettes, snuff, chewing tobacco, household items and groceries without money the store owner would just write what my parents owed in a book and my father would go by and make payments on Friday's. Most of the time the adults used me as a runner to run errands to the store and give me 50 cents or a dollar which added up after several trips.

After my mother and father constantly being separated, After seeing this go on time and time again, I finally drove my dad to work one morning, kept his car and while he was at work I got a couple of my football friends I used his car and we got a truck packed up our things and moved my mother out for good. To this day, my father is now deceased I never knew if till the day he ever knew I was the one who packed up and moved my mother away.

At age 18, I graduated from high school and entered the military the United States Army shortly after graduation.

MY ADULTHOOD

My name is Thomas Leonard Mitchell; I have two nicknames Leon and Mitch.

I am married and have four kids. I have three grandchildren. I reside in Wentzville Missouri. I own and manage a bodyguard / protection, security and Investigations company called Comfort Zone Security, Protection & Investigations, LLC. I am a trendsetter and have been a business owner for 14 years. I have worked in all four Government Municipalities City, County, State and Federal.

I have been very active in church and community events, I enjoy spending time with family and friends. However once you get to know me, depending on the moment I can be sweet and sarcastic, democratic and authoritarian, flexible and at times stiffed-necked. I pride myself as possessing a strong resume in being a people's person and public servant. I must say that of all my training, academies I have attended, schools I have attended has equipped me with the tools to be a surviver. My philosophy is this it really does not matter if I live in the country or big city, it does not matter if I drink out of a jelly jar or the finest crystal, plastic ware or sterling silver, lie on a cushy sofa or lay on a cot. I learned to treat every situation and chance that comes my way as an opportunity. My hobbies are I enjoy spending time and taking vacations with my family, going dancing, horseback riding, basketball, football, swimming, racquetball, going shooting at the range. But really I just enjoy the simple things in life.

MY EXTENDED FAMILY MEMBERS

My father John Thomas Mitchell –occupation was a welder

My Father's side of the family is the Mitchell's

Grandfather-Henry Oneal Mitchell-(Deceased)
Grandmother- Rosa Mitchell-(Deceased)

My Grandparents they had 13 children:

Sons-John Thomas (Deceased), David, Sterling, Terry, Lamar (Deceased), Ralph (Deceased) Henry Jr (Deceased)

Daughters-Mary, Shirley, Rene (Deceased) Brenda (Deceased), Sara Jo (Deceased) Bertha (Deceased)

My mother Sue Nell Mitchell—occupation was a seamstress

My mother's side of the family is the McCurry's

Grandfather-RJ McCurry (Deceased)

Grandmother-Helen McCurry (Deceased)

My Grandparents they had 7 children:

Sons- Paul-(Deceased) Curtis, James

Daughters-Virginia(Deceased), Sue, Louise, Diane

As far as I know all my family members lives in Georgia, South Carolina and Chicago

MY IMMEDIATE FAMILY

Father: Thomas L. Mitchell (Myself)

Mother: Karen Denise Mitchell (Brown)

Sons: Thomas L. Mitchell Jr & Tyren L. Mitchell

Daughters: Tanisha N. Mitchell & Karis D. Mitchell

Grand Children(s): Sophee Conrad Mitchell (Father is Thomas Jr.)
Leo Thomas Mitchell (Father is Tyren)
Tacar Enrique Mitchell (Father Thomas Jr.)

MY JOBS AND OCCUPATIONS

I have worked in all four government municipalities: City, County, State & Federal

Owner/Operator, *Comfort Zone Security, Protection & Investigations, LLC, Lake St. Louis, MO*

06/2006 ----Present

I am responsible for the day to day management and operation of a full service dignitary/ executive protection and private investigations company. I am a Private Investigator licensed by the State of Missouri. I am a Top Rated Specialist in intelligence based executive protection High and Low profile operations. "An ounce of prevention saves a pound of cure." Benjamin Franklin

I have worked in all aspects of the security field including Executive Protection, Celebrity Protection, High Profile operations, Low Profile operations, Venue, Concerts, Events, Press Junkets, Premier Red Carpets and Residential security. I have worked as a Solo Bodyguard for both "A" list Entertainment Professionals and Fortune 500 Executives. I specialize in armed and unarmed low profile operations.

XFL Security Representative / Consultant, Stamford CT

December 2019—April 2020

Executive Level Consultant responsible for overall team and venue security. Responsible for coordinating all aspects of security for the XFL league at team level, assisting in developing, planning, and implementing security programs, in addition to directing emergency response, risk assessments, event planning and security strategies for the XFL and its teams. Responsible for providing investigative and security services, including consulting, general investigation and information gathering, stadium security, crowd management and crowd control. Additionally, responsible for assisting in the coordination of game day team and stadium security to include coordinating security at high-profile, scheduled events attended by players, coaches and staff.

Lieutenant, Moscow Mills Police Department, Moscow Mills Missouri

08/2009-------Retired 12/2019

I Directs and leads subordinates in enforcing laws and ordinances for the Police Department. Supervises, evaluates, trains and provides guidance to subordinate personnel. Communicates and maintains good relations with the general public, city officials and other law enforcement agencies. Assist the Chief of Police with the management of the reserve program. Interprets policies and procedures for application and interprets laws, ordinances and court decisions relating to enforcement activities.

Field Investigator, Litigation Solutions, Pittsburgh, PA

01/2016----07/2017

I was responsible for conducting field work investigations for work compensation cases.

Contract Inspector, National Creditor Connection, Inc. (NCCI), Lake Forest, California

10/2011----08/2013

I was responsible for conducting field work investigations and inspections on businesses that require data base services from Clients.

Contract Investigator, Key Point Government Solutions / Office of Personnel Management,

Loveland, Colorado------05/2009-----12/2011

I served as a contract investigator retained by the Federal Investigative Services, and the U.S. Office of Personnel Management to conduct Background, Civil Service and National Security Investigations.

Event Manager, the Family Arena, St. Charles, Missouri

07/2006 – 04/2015

I was responsible for the daily operation of the 10,000 seats Arena. I am Responsible for the hiring, training and supervising over 150 employees which consists of Ushers, Ticket Takers, Collectors, Parking Attendants and Crowd Management. Create monthly schedules for staffing, coordinate with Human Resources/ Payroll Department regarding all aspects of employee personnel data, i.e. address changes, pay rates, Tax W-2 paper work and punch time cards for employees. I coordinate with the local Sheriff Department and Medical Paramedics to schedule personnel for each event. Communicate with the Director of the Family Arena and Departmental staff for proper staffing and Event Preparation. Respond to any problems and / or requests for assistance from event staff, including any disturbances and/or guests attempting to enter the building with prohibited items, emergency situations and other general concerns. Prepare attendance and labor reports for show settlement and oversee all guest service aspects during an event, including customer safety and enjoyment.

Federal Air Marshal, Department of Homeland Security, Transportation Security Administration, Armonk New York, 1/2004 – 05/2006

I was responsible for providing security and protection or Air Security in an effort to detect, deter, and defeat hostile acts targeting the U.S., U.S. Carriers, Airports, Passengers and Crew Members.

Director of Loss Prevention and Safety, Omni Hotels,

Las Colinas, TX, 10/2003 - 1/2004

I Directed the Security Department's day-to-day operations. I supervised a staff of eight officers and one supervisor. I implemented and trained staff on the Occupational Safety Health Act. I Coordinated and administered the Safety/ Security programs for the Hotel. I maintained an effective Key Control Program. I trained and certified staff on Blood borne Pathogens and CPR. I am knowledgeable on liability and labor laws and coordinated claims through corporate Office.

Security Forces Police Supervisor, United States Air Force National Guard, Memphis, TN,

1/1995 - 11/1999

I supervised a shift of Security Policeman that patrolled the military installation for criminal activity, provided technical support and direction on the proper use of the Units CCTV and Access Control Equipment. I investigated crimes on the installations pertaining to personal and property crimes. I provided security and assisted the United States Secret Service in handling protection for the President and Vice President of the United States of America. I enforced Air Force laws and regulations. I was the primary trainer in physical and area security. I performed additional duties as an **Air Force Phoenix Raven** which included flying armed on military aircraft providing global security and protection for the crew members, equipment and aircraft.

Sex Crimes Detective, City of Memphis Police Department, Memphis, TN,

12/1992 - 4/2003

I investigated adult and child abuse cases. Interviewed and obtained statements. I processed, preserved and presented physical evidence in court proceedings. I conducted line-ups and obtained warrants for arrest. I also worked with other agencies with divorces, custody battles, and protective custody hearings.

Correctional Officer, Shelby County Corrections, Memphis, TN,

7/1991 - 12/1992

I was responsible for the security of inmates in a medium security prison. I supervised inmates during recreation, visitation and within the housing areas. I transported inmates to appropriate appointments locations away from prison grounds.

Correctional Sergeant, Texas Department of Corrections, Huntsville, TX,

10/1989 - 6/1991

I performed the role of a Building Sergeant for a 2,500 medium security prison. I supervised five Correctional Officers, trained officers on physical and area security and overall prison awareness.

Operations/Platoon Sergeant, United States Army, Fort Hood, TX,

8/1981 - 9/1989

I directed operations for the largest Ammunition Supply Point in the United States, which consisted of 400 acres including 57 warehouses containing stocks valued at 39 million dollars. Supervised over 100 military and civilian personnel, was responsible for the continued success, training, health, morale, welfare and development of all personnel. I helped developed, managed, and executed the ammunition surety program. I supervised the storage, receipt, issue, maintenance, stock control and accounting of ammunition and components. I implemented an innovative space utilization and inventory program for the warehouses that stored the ammunition and components.

MY High School Jobs: Working in a textile mill called Dunlap where we produced tennis balls, I worked in the summer for the Corps of Engineers going out with teams to parks to work on signs, picnic grills, latern poles and spray weed killer on the grass and weeds. I worked at a local chicken factory where I collected the eggs and lastly I picked cotton to earn money. I cut grass and raked leaves for different people to make extra money.

MILITARY SERVICE, ASSIGNMENTS & TRAVELS

I SERVED IN THREE DIFFERENT MILITARY BRANCHES

I served in the United States Army:

Rank: Staff Sergeant- E-6-MOS-- Ammunition Specialist

I was stationed at Fort Leonard wood Missouri (Basic Training), Redstone Arsenal, Huntsville, Alabama Advanced Individual Training (AIT), The Ammunition and Munitions Center, Fort Steward, Georgia, Hunter Army Airfield Savannah, Georgia, Fort Irwin, San Bernardino, California, Fort Hood, Killeen, Texas

Foreign Countries: Wildflecken Germany (Two Tours),

I served in the United States Air Force National Guard:

Rank: Technical Sergeant E-6—MOS- Security Police

I was stationed at Lackland Air Force Base, San Antonio, Texas, Tennessee Air National Guard, Memphis, Tennessee, Travis Air Force Base, Fairfield, California,

Foreign Countries: Panama, Lima Peru, Chile, Argentina

I served in the United States Air Force Reserves:

Rank: Technical Sergeant E-6—MOS –Supply Sergeant

I was stationed at Whiteman Air Force Base, Warrensburg, Missouri

MY CIVILIAN TRAVELS STATESIDE & OVERSEAS

OVERSEAS: Spain, Amsterdam, Holland, Australia, London, Monterrey Mexico, Canada, Rome, Doho Qatar, Beirut Lebanon, and Turkey

Stateside: Visited all of the 50 U.S. States: Alabama (AL) - Montgomery Alaska (AK) - Juneau Arizona (AZ) - Phoenix Arkansas (AR) - Little Rock California (CA) - Sacramento Colorado (CO) - Denver Connecticut (CT) - Hartford Delaware (DE) - Dover Florida (FL) - Tallahassee Georgia (GA) - Atlanta Hawaii (HI) - Honolulu Idaho (ID) - Boise Illinois (IL) - Springfield Indiana (IN) - Indianapolis Iowa (IA) - Des Moines Kansas (KS) - Topeka Kentucky (KY) - Frankfort Louisiana (LA) - Baton Rouge Maine (ME) - Augusta Maryland (MD) - Annapolis Massachusetts

(MA)- Boston Michigan (MI) - Lansing Minnesota (MN) - St. Paul Mississippi (MS) - Jackson Missouri (MO) - Jefferson City Montana (MT) - Helena Nebraska (NE)- Lincoln Nevada (NV) – Carson City New Hampshire (NH) - Concord New Jersey (NJ) - Trenton New Mexico (NM) - Santa Fe New York (NY) - Albany North Carolina (NC) - Raleigh North Dakota (ND) - Bismarck Ohio (OH) - Columbus Oklahoma (OK) - Oklahoma City Oregon (OR) - Salem Pennsylvania (PA) - Harrisburg Rhode Island (RI) - Providence South Carolina (SC) - Columbia South Dakota (SD) - Pierre Tennessee (TN) - Nashville Texas (TX) - Austin Utah (UT) - Salt Lake City Vermont (VT) - Montpelier Virginia (VA) - Richmond Washington (WA) - Olympia West Virginia (WV) - Charleston Wisconsin (WI) - Madison Wyoming (WY) – Cheyenne

MY CIVILIAN/MILITARY EDUCATION

*Candidate BS, Organizational Leadership and Counseling, University of Memphis, TN, 12/2020—two classes left

* Associate Degree in Criminal Justice, Central Texas College, Killeen, TX, 1988

* Certification in Paralegal Studies, School of Paralegal Studies, Boca Raton, FL, 1991

MY MOST MEMORABLE
LESSONS & EXPERIENCES

My highlights and most memberable experiences serving in the Army were:

- When I met my wife and her family (especially my mother-in-law the late Hattie Mae Brown)
- My first daughter was born Tanisha Nicole Mitchell aka "Nikki"
- My first son was born Thomas L Mitchell Jr. aka "Tank"
- I joined the free Masonic Lodge
- Traveling to different countries meeting real nice people and making friendships along the way
- Coaching a dependent youth activities football pee wee league while station in Wildflecken Germany, where

I coached who is now a famous NBA pro basketball player, Shaquille O'Neal aka Shaq

In 1989, after leaving the U.S. Army, I was hired by the Texas Department of Corrections as a Correctional Officer 1. I went through the Corrections Academy in Huntsville, Texas, after graduating; I was assigned to the Beto # 1 Unit in Palestine Texas, which was a 2, 2000 bed maximum security Male prison. After completing a year of probation, I requested a hardship transfer to the Alfred Hughes Unit, located in Gatesville, Texas. This prison was closer to Fort Hood Texas because my family was still living there due to my wife being a military officer (Captain) still stationed at Fort hood. I resigned from the prison industry in 1992. I achieved the rank of correctional officer 111.

My highlights and most memberable experiences working in the State of Texas Prison System were:

- **The experience of being locked up, when you are not the one doing the time.
- *The experience of understanding the society of people that were incarcerated.
- The experience of seeing first had in and outs of prison life, EVENTHOUGH I was not the police officer who

put them in jail, nor the attorney who represented them or the judge that sentenced them. I had no right to judge them on the crime(s) they committed or accused of committing. I learned that If you wanted to be respected you must also give respect regardless keeping in mind they are serving time without being eligible for parole or a life sentence, so they have nothing to lose

- The benefits and services inmates receive despite of being locked down
- Meeting with talented inmates that were very gifted in crafts and woodwork.
- Meeting good co workers and friends
- I was very amazed by the State of Texas Prison System, because each prison specializes in a certain industry. The inmates do all the work either they grow, make, build and transport everything that it takes to operate a prison. The first prison I worked at was Beto #1 Unit it specialized in the Poultry and Meat Factory.; they supplied the meat and poultry to the other Texas prisons with those items. The second prison I worked at was the Alfred Hughes Unit, it specialized in the Garment Factory made all the inmates uniforms for all the prisons and all the correctional officers' uniforms for all the prisons. The Sign Shop made all the highway signs, street signs and vehicle tags for the

State of Texas. Each prison had tractor and trailers that transported orders of supplies that each prison request to their prison. The inmate drives the truck and the correctional officer ride shotgun.

In 1991, I was contacted by a company called Brown & Root located in Houston, Texas. They had left a message on my house phone stating that they had a contract from the United States Forces. The contract was to pack up and ship all ammunition that was left over in Saudi Arabia from Desert Shield and Desert Storm which needed to be shipped back to the United States. They stated that they were looking for recently discharged military personnel that were recently left the military whom had experience in the ammunition field and they pulled my name out of a database. So I accepted the job offer as a Packaging and Preservation Supervisor and signed a contract with this company. I was sent to Al Khobar and Dhahran, I lived in a villa, I was assigned my own land rover vehicle and a 16 man team third country nationals and an interpreter to work for me. I had to train, teach and care for my crew. Our mission was to check, clean, sort and package serviceable and non- serviceable ammunition and ship it back to the United States. Also any ammunition that was non serviceable we had to conduct Emergency Ordinance Disposal (EOD) procedures.

My highlights and most memberable experiences working in the State of Texas Prison System were:

- It was definitely one of the longest flights I had ever flown
- Seeing the way Arabic versus Non Arabic people were treated
- Observing and seeing so many Mosques, Pyramids and Camels
- The lessons I learned from my crew in regards to the lessons I taught my crew

In 1992, I returned from Saudi Arabia. I was reunited with my family in Texas. Shortly afterwards we relocated to Memphis, TN due to my wife completing her military obligation and accepting a job with a company there.

In 1992, we moved to Memphis, TN and I applied for jobs to several agencies, The City of Memphis Police Department, Shelby County Sheriff Department and Shelby County Corrections. The first agency that called me was Shelby County Correction known as the Penal Farm, I worked there for approximately eleven months as a Correctional Officer, after receiving a call from the Memphis Police Department, I accepted the job and started the Memphis Police Department Training academy in August 1993 and served for eleven years.

My highlights and most rememberable experiences working at the Shelby County Corrections facility were:

- Being able to see firsthand the major differences between the Texas Prison System and the Tennessee Prison System

In 1994, while as a Police Officer, I joined the Tennessee Air Force National Guard, I went to training at Lackland Air force Base, located in San Antonio, Texas. I trained as a Security Police and later a Phoenix Raven traveling armed on C130 and C141 aircrafts on flights across Central and South America. I flew in Hot Zones such as Chile, Argentina, Panama and Lima Peru. I served five years.

My highlights and most memberable experiences working at Tennessee Air National Guard were:

- Travelling
- Being able to experience two different branches of service
- The people I have met and are still friends until this day

- Being a member of the President and Vice President of America Protection Details
- Guarding and Taking a tour on Air force #1—President Bill Clinton

My highlights and most rememberable experiences working at Memphis Police Department were:

- The birth of my second son Tyren L Mitchell aka "Tray"
- The birth of my youngest daughter Karis D Mitchell aka "KeKe"
- The assignments that I had the opportunity to work in and grow in my Law Enforcement career such as Community Based Policing, Sex Crimes Detective, CIT Instructor, Neighborhood Watch Trainer and Mounted Patrol

In 2001 while working as a Sex Crime Detective for the Memphis, TN Police, I was sitting at my desk I remember one of my co-workers saying hey Detective Mitchell come here for a minute, so I got up went in the break room and he said a airplane just hit the World Trade Center Tower in New York, I responded WOW the pilot must have been drunk or fell asleep. Before I could walk out of the room a second plane hit the other tower that became known as the Twin Towers. So over the next couple of days and weeks at that time President George W Bush was President and he stated that America was afraid to fly and not having airplanes in the air was crippling America and he enacted a new federal Agency called the Department of Homeland Security. He further stated he was looking for Federal Air Marshals (Sky Marshals) I went home discussed my desire to be an Air Marshal with my wife and she gave me her blessings. In 2003, I resigned from the Memphis Police Department and moved to Dallas, Texas via Mesquite Texas my wife transferred there for a promotion. While I was waiting on my training date and my Top Secret Clearance to come back. I got a job with the Hotels chain called Omni Hotels as the Director of Loss Prevention and Safety however four months into the job I received my training date. I resigned and I attended training in Artesia, New Mexico and Advanced training in Atlantic City New Jersey. After graduation I was assigned to the New York Field Office in Armonk New York. I took flights out of JFK, LaGuardia and Newark. I resigned in 2006 and started my own Bodyguard, Security and Investigations company called Comfort Zone Security, Protection & Investigations, LLC.

My highlights and most memorable experiences working at Department of Homeland Security were:

- The high tech state of the training
- Meeting so many fellow FAMs from other field offices
- Traveling across the globe
- Keeping America Safe

In 2009, since I was trained and conditioned to carrying a gun and badge for over 30 plus years, I went to the Chief of Police in Moscow Mills Police Department in Moscow Mills Missouri and asked him can he use a professional to assist in the department. He hired me on the spot, I was hired as the Lieutenant over the reserves. I was sworn in by the Mayor and served for 10 years and recently retired on September 1, 2019.

My highlights and most memorable experiences working at the Moscow Mills Police Department were:

- The difference between a city department and a rural small town department
- The first time I attended court and heard the judge fine a person for cat at large
- Ten dollars for each piece of wood a guy stole from a general store
- Retirement

MY ONCE IN A LIFETIME EXPERIENCES

- Guarding and taking a tour on Air force # 1 Plane-Vice President Bill Clinton
- Guarding and taking a tour on Air force # 2 Plane –Vice President Al Gore
- Being part of the protection details for the President and Vice President of US
- Sitting in while in sessions of the Senate and House of Representatives
- Worked security at the Kayak Venue for the 1996 Olympics
- Sign a contract with Colors Talent Agency for modeling and acting

- Played as an extra with a speaking part the following films/ movies:

  The Rainmaker-Police officer-Constellation Films/ Director Francis Ford Coppola

  The Firm—Correctional Officer- Paramount Motion Pictures/Director Sydney Pollack

  21 Grams-Police Detective- Universal Studios/director Alejandro G. Inarrigu

- Played as a principle in the following commercials:
- Xenedrine- Basketball Player –McCrary Productions/ Director Bob McCrary
- Lubiscuit-Security Officer for Pau Gasol --Dichotomy Films/Director John Barreiro
- Mr. Pride Car Wash-Police Officer- Mr. Pride Incorporation /Director Larry Wheeler

MY CERTIFICATIONS/ TRAINING / LICENSES

FLETC Basic law Enforcement training; Private Investigator, Certified Protection Professional Training; Guest Services Professional certification; Federal Air Marshal Training; Firearms; Physical Techniques; Law; Report Writing; Use of Force; Tactics; OPSEC; Weapons of Mass Destruction; Bombs& Explosives; Fingerprint Lab; Courtroom Testimony; Personal Protection; Officer Liability; Defensive Tactics and Verbal Judo, Jail Basic Training Course, Correctional Officer Academy, Memphis Police Department Basic Police Academy, Neighborhood Watch Instructor Training, Citizen Police Academy, Sex Crimes and Homicides Advanced Investigative Techniques; Street Gangs Seminar; Drug Interdiction for Patrols; CIT Trainer Instructor; Street Survival Seminar; Neighborhood Watch Instructor; Crisis

Intervention Team Instructor Training, Hostage Negotiator Training, Behavioral Crime Scene Analysis, United States Air Force Law Enforcement Apprentice Course, United States Army Missile and Munitions Training, The Reid Technique in Interviewing and Interrogation, The Reid Technique in Advanced Interviewing and Interrogation. Trained in anti-hijacking/anti-terrorism and intelligence research.

MY AWARDS AND ACCOMODATIONS

1999 National Alliance of mentally ill Appreciation Award

1999 Awarded Life Saving Medal

1999 Certificate of Appreciation for the Olympics

1999 Nominated for Officer of the Month

1998 Nominated for CIT Officer of the Year

U.S. Army Good Conduct Medal

U.S. Army Meritorious Service Medal

U.S. Army Achievement Medal

U.S. Army Honorable Discharge

U.S. Air force National Guard Honorable Discharge

U.S. Air force Reserve Honorable Discharge

Numerous Letters of Commendations & Certificates of Appreciation

MY POEMS AND INSPIRATIONS

COME TAKE A RIDE WITH ME

Come take a ride with me to a place you have never been
Come take a ride with me and travel to an endless end
Come take a ride with me, get ready to go, see and do
Come take a ride with me get inside a place within you
Come take a ride with me, now we are slowing down
    almost sitting still
Come take a ride with me, It was the moving of the
    mind not wheels

FOR THE LOVE OF IT

For the love of it is what I say when everything is going
my way

For the love of it is how I feel when all my desires
appears so real

For the love of it is believing that there is no other way

For the love of it is wakening up to face another day

For the love of it is always, is always a good approach to
all my inner strengths

For the love of it is the joy that I have my mind, body
and soul intense

For the love of it is all my blessings I receive from the
Lord above

For the love of it are the grace and mercy and Gods
unchanging love

DO YOU KNOW WHO I AM?
HERE IS MY ANSWER

I AM ONE OF A KIND

"ME"

I am the only "me" I've got. I am unique. There are two major parts of me. There is the inside "me" and the outside "me". The outside me is what you see. The way I act, the image I portray, the way I look and the things I do. The outside me is very important. It is my messenger to the world and much of my outside me is what communicates with you. I value what I have done, the way I look, and what I share with you. The inside "me" knows all my feelings, my secrets ideas, and my many hopes and dreams.

Sometimes I let you know a little bit about the inside "me" and sometimes it's a very private part of myself.

Even though there are an enormous number of people in this world, no one is exactly like "me". I take full responsibility for "me" and the more I learn about myself, the more responsibility I am going to take. You see, my "me" is my responsibility. As I know myself more and more, I find out that I am an OK person. I've done some good things in my life because I am a good person. I have accomplished some things in my life because I am a competent person. I know some special people because I am worth knowing. I celebrate the many things I have done for myself.

I've also made some mistakes. I can learn from them. I have also known some people who did not appreciate me. I do not need to keep those people in my life. I've wasted some precious time. I can make new choices now. As long as I can see, hear, feel, think, change, grow, and behave, I have great possibility. I'm going to take those risks and those possibilities, and I am going to grow, and love and be and celebrate. I am worth it.

"Unknown"

CONCLUSION

Well I have told you my life story; I have shared with you my ups, downs, triumphs, accomplishment, highlights of my life and my inner feelings. The WORLD (United States of America) does not stop and wait on nobody. I can only be truthful to the best that I can be, is there social justice, universal justice on this earth? Maybe!!! Or maybe not you have to be the judge of that.

The world we live in is certainly uncertain. It is unfair but people do succeed, they chase and follow their dreams like I did. Some people become the movie stars, professional athletes, politician, the teachers, the scientists, the business owner, the POTUS!!!!!!!!!!!!! Let's focus on the President of the United States job for a moment, there is no standard ; there is no requirement, no qualifications for this person to become a power figure and rule the world.

This person becomes the Commander and Chief, this person starts wars, this person change religions and this person operate on their own agendas. It is easy to succeed in life being prominent, dishonest, and treacherous and use your position and office for personal gain. This person die rich, appears to be happy and successful, this person live to be really old.

I believe in order to make this world a better place we as people need to start caring again, be honest people, be kind and mindful people, take an interest and truly care about what happens to humankind regardless of race, gender or origin. Because at the end of the day we are all we got. We are so much alike than we are different when it comes to looks, habits, wants and desires. We all breathe the same air and **Maslow Eight Theories** For Living is <u>Physiological needs</u> the need for air, water, food, sleep, shelter, and clothing. <u>Safety needs</u> the need for protection from elements, security, order, law, stability, freedom and from fear. <u>Belonging needs</u> the need for social, emotionally based relationships, sexual intimacy, and having supportive and communicative family. <u>Self-Esteem needs</u>, the need to be respected, self respect and to respect others, to feel accepted and self valued to be in a profession or hobby. <u>Cognitive needs</u> the need to increase your intelligence and chase knowledge, the need to learn, explore, discover and create to get a better understanding of the world around you. <u>Aesthetic needs</u> the need for humans to need beautiful imagery or something new and aesthetically pleasing and to refresh themselves. <u>Self-Actualization needs</u> the need instinctual need for humans to make the most of their abilities and to strive to be the best they can be basically the feeling of generatively. <u>Self-Transcendence needs</u>, <u>Spiritual needs</u>, the need to find meaning, the feeling of integrity, having purpose and value in your life, such needs can or cannot be specifically religious, but even people who have no religious preference or faith or not a member of an organized body or have a belief system they still require something to give them meaning and purpose.

So I feel that people that are racist and show prejudice is downright mean, depraved and crazy only TIME can change that. They have to just die off because a new generation has come. Every race have the same people doing the same jobs, every race have people marrying into different races. So <u>Time</u> is the key to unlock the door.

<u>Time </u>in my opinion is the most valuable commodity we have as people, let's look at this thing called TIME, we all have the same 365 Days in a year, the same 24 hours in a Day, the same 1,440 minutes in a Day, the same 86,400 Seconds in a Day.

The problem is not <u>Time</u> but what are you doing with your <u>Time</u> that you have been given. A billionaire cannot buy you more time, A doctor cannot prescribe you more time, a judge cannot grant you more time, a seamstress cannot sew you more time, a farmer cannot grow you more time, an author cannot write you more time, a builder cannot build you more time. Nobody can REFUND you more time, you cannot get a refund or inherit your time back from wasting your time on people that are or were ungrateful of your time. You cannot get a refund back on your time wasted in a bad relationship, a bad marriage, wasted on a dead end job, wasted in school without a plan. Hanging out in bars, clubs and events those are called memories.

So <u>TIME</u> is Valuable and should never be wasted, not even one second. For example fairly sized supermarkets or grocery stores have perishable and non perishable items. Each item have a date stamped on it some are called Due dates or Expiration dates. So what that means is that item must be consumed or used by that date or it will be taken off the shelf or container. We as human beings also have a due date stamped on each one of us called DEATH which is unknown but trust me you have a due date stamped on you which means that you should consume the best life as a person, do the best you can as a person; because one day you will be taken off as your earth life will expire and thou will be taken off the shelf of life.

So I have observed in every grave yard; I have seen tombstones; they all have a born date and a death date it looks something like this John T Doe January 1, 1900-July 5, 1990 that dash between the two dates tells everyone while you were living what you have done, who you helped, what impact you had while on EARTH. The Dash not the Born date but the DASH not the Death date but the Dash.

What will be your LEGACY be? What will your DASH tell everyone? In closing hope I succeeded in my quest to show you my Dash even though my death date is not yet came as I write this book.

Please remember no one owns anything in this world; we only occupy and enjoy our homes, cars, jobs, worldly possessions for now, though we don't like to think about it all but all of us will encounter the due date one day, no funeral possession ever have u hauls, or moving trucks following behind; you cannot take any of those things with you when you die. So quit being so possessive and controlling, give if you can, share if you have extra, help when you should GREED is the enemy. Now that you know who I AM

Thank you for making it through the end of" Do You Know Who I Am". I hope it was informative and I provided you with some insights to achieve your goals whatever they may be. I hope you can now take the necessary steps to be all you can be and live your best life. I pray and wish you success in any road your journey might take you.

Sincerely,
Mitch

MY JOURNEY: MY TRAINING--- MY TRAVELS- MY
TALENTS—MY TIME— MY THOUGHTS—

MY TEACHINGS--MY TRUTHS— MY

TENACITY- MY TIREDNESS—MY TRACE--

MY TRIALS— MY THEORY-- MY

TRIBLATIONS-- MY TRIUMPHS—MY TASTE

MY "THANKS"

08/1981—09/1989 — United States Army
10/1989—06/1991 — Texas Department of Criminal Justice
07/1991—12/1992 — Shelby County Corrections
12/1992—04/2013 — United States Air Force
01/1995—11/1999 — United States Air Force
01/1995—11/1999 — United States Air Force
01/1997—11/1999 — United States Air Force
01/2004—05/2006 — United Stares Federal Air Marshal
06/2006—Present — Comfort Zone Security